THE MESS

by
Dalen Keys

Illustrated by Kim Sponaugle

THE MESS
Copyright © 2011 Dalen Keys
ISBN 978-1-886068-50-6
Library of Congress Control Number: 2011936424

Published by Fruitbearer Publishing, LLC
P.O. Box 777, Georgetown, DE 19947
(302) 856-6649 • FAX (302) 856-7742
www.fruitbearer.com • info@fruitbearer.com
Illustrated by Kim Sponaugle
Edited by Pam Halter

Printed in the United States of America
by BookMasters, Inc.
30 Amberwood Parkway, Ashland, OH 44805
October 2011 • Job #M8905

DEDICATED TO

the real dancing Tiffany
and the real quilting Mommy.

Tiffany danced across her room tightly hugging her favorite doll.

She twirled around a pile of dirty clothes, leaped over a tea set scattered across the floor, and gracefully pirouetted before she stopped in front of her bookshelf.

"This is your special place, Carrie," Tiffany said as she placed her doll on a shelf next to a piggy bank. "You sit right there and be a good girl!"

"Are you cleaning your room?" Mommy said as she stepped into Tiffany's room.

"Yes, I am. Can't you tell?"

"I wasn't exactly sure," Mommy said. "I thought maybe you were just dancing."

Tiffany giggled. "Can't I do both?"

"I guess so, but don't forget to pick up your dirty clothes."

"I will, Mommy. I promise!"

Mommy kissed Tiffany on the top of her head. "I'll be in my quilting room if you need me. I'm working on a new quilt."

Tiffany picked up her dirty jeans. "Okay, Mommy. Can I come see it when I'm done?"

"You bet! I'd like to know if you like it," Mommy said.

Mommy stopped sewing as Tiffany soon skipped into the room. "Did you finish cleaning your room already?"

"Kind of."

Mommy frowned. "Uh, oh. That sounds like you've got more to do."

"Just a little, but I really needed a break, Mommy! I was fraggled and plustrated."

Mommy smiled. "I think you were probably frazzled and frustrated."

Tiffany nodded.

"Yes, I was!"

"Why were you frazzled and frustrated?" Mommy asked as Tiffany sat on her lap..

"My doll wanted all my attention when I really needed to be cleaning up my room."

Mommy hugged Tiffany tightly. "I certainly understand. Do you want to stay in here with me for a little while?"

Tiffany nodded making her pigtails bounce.

Tiffany looked around Mommy's quilting room. "I think you need to clean up your room, too."

"I do?"

Tiffany shook her finger at Mommy. "Yes, you do. It's a mess in here!"

Mommy looked around the room. "I think you are right. Sometimes my special doll wants all my attention too."

"Where's your special doll?" asked Tiffany looking from side to side.

Mommy winked at her. "She's sitting on my lap."

"Who?" said Tiffany. "Me?"

Tiffany slid off Mommy's lap and knelt beside a stack of old clothes on the floor. "Are these my old jeans?"

"Yes they are. Someday I am going to make a quilt from those old clothes—including your old jeans."

Tiffany wrinkled her nose. "But why?"

"I hate to throw away old clothes when I can make a beautiful quilt out of them," Mommy said. "Then every time I see the quilt, I'll remember the people who wore those clothes."

"Even me?" Tiffany said.

"Especially you!"

After three big hops, two small jumps, and one step, Tiffany stood beside a worktable with quilt blocks spread across it. "I like these quilt blocks, Mommy! They look like big friendly spiders."

Mommy smiled. "I'm glad you like them because I'm making them into a quilt for you."

"Really?" said Tiffany picking up one of the blocks. "Yippee! I like spiders."

Mommy shivered. "I know, dear, and I really don't understand why. You must get that from your daddy."

Tiffany crawled under the worktable into a row between shelves stacked high with colorful fabrics. She pushed aside some fabric hanging down from above. "I'll be exploring in the deep, dark jungle, Mommy."

"Okay, dear, be careful. Who knows what might be in there. Let me know if you find any treasures."

"Treasure? Cool!" Tiffany said as she turned to enter the mysterious jungle.

Thick trees hung overhead as Tiffany crawled into the dim light of the fabric jungle. She froze when she caught a glimpse of something on the path directly ahead of her. She inched forward as eerie cries of wild animals rang out from deep within the jungle.

"I can't tell what it is," she whispered as she stopped beside a strange little mound. She held her breath as she leaned closer. "I think it's a little hedgehog who's taking a nap."

Just then, the hedgehog awoke and blinked its sleepy eyes. "Who are you?" asked the hedgehog.

"I'm Tiffany. Who are you?"

"I'm Mr. Cushion," said the hedgehog. "I'm lost. Can you help me?"

Tiffany carefully picked up Mr. Cushion. "Yes, I can. We'll get out of this jungle together."

"Thank you very much!" Mr. Cushion said.

Mr. Cushion and Tiffany suddenly peeked over the edge of Mommy's sewing table making her jump. "This is Mr. Cushion," Tiffany said. "He was lost in the dark jungle."

"Oh! You scared me, Mr. Cushion," Mommy said.

Tiffany put Mr. Cushion next to her ear. "He's kind of shy but he said he's sorry."

"I wondered where you were, Mr. Cushion," said Mommy. "I'm glad to see you again."

Tiffany looked at Mr. Cushion and nodded. "He's glad to see you again, too."

"He can sit right here next to my sewing machine," Mommy said. "But no more exploring in the jungle, young man."

Tiffany set Mr. Cushion on the table. "He said okay. It was scary in there anyway."

Tiffany watched Mommy sewing another spider quilt block. "Can I use your sewing machine sometime?"

"I'd be happy to teach you. Do you want to be a quilter?"

"I think so," Tiffany said as she wrapped a beautiful piece of green and yellow fabric around her shoulders. "Will I be able to use a sewing machine?"

"One of your very own," said Mommy.

"Will I be able to have my own quilting room too?"

"Of course!"

Tiffany smiled. "Can mine be messy like yours?"

Mommy frowned. "Ouch! That hurt."

Tiffany twirled toward the door but stopped suddenly. "Mommy?"

"Yes, dear?"

Tiffany put her hands on her hips. "This room is still a mess and you have to clean it up before you can play!"

"Are you grounding me?"

Tiffany smiled. "Yes I am!"

Mommy held up a spider block. "But beautiful things come out of all this mess."

"Like spiders!" Tiffany said.

"Yuck!" Mommy said. "I meant quilts."

"Mommy, something beautiful comes out of the mess in my room too."

"Really? Like what?"

Tiffany skipped across the room and gave Mommy a big hug. "Me!"

Mommy laughed. "You're absolutely right, dear. But you still have to pick up your dirty clothes."

TO ORDER

Visit www.dalenkeys.com or send your name, address, phone number, and e-mail (if applicable), with $16.00 per book + $5.95 S/H to:

Dalen Keys
260 Fern Ridge
Landenberg, PA 19350

Please make checks payable to Dalen Keys.

If you are interested in having your book(s) autographed, please include the name(s) you want inscribed.

Questions? Call (484) 889-9125
email dkeystone@comcast.net

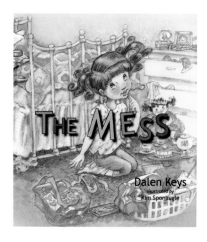

www.fruitbearer.com